D1614604

PIANO CONCERTO HIGHLIGHTS

for Solo Piano

Edited by
FELIX GUENTHER

DOVER PUBLICATIONS, INC.
Mineola, New York

Bibliographical Note

This Dover edition, first published in 2006, is an unabridged republication of
The Heart of the Piano Concerto, originally published by Mercury Music Corp.,
New York, n.d. Musical cues corresponding to cuts on an accompanying recording
have been omitted.

International Standard Book Number: 0-486-44958-0

Manufactured in the United States of America
Dover Publications, Inc., 31 East 2nd Street, Mineola, N.Y. 11501

CONTENTS

PIANO CONCERTO IN D MINOR

2nd & 3rd Movement

J. S. Bach

Allegro. (♩ = 108.) (Condensed)

PIANO CONCERTO IN D MINOR
(K. 466)
2nd Movement

W. A. Mozart

Romanze.

PIANO CONCERTO No. 3

In C Minor—1st Movement

L. van Beethoven

Allegro con brio

30

PIANO CONCERTO IN A MINOR

2nd Movement

R. Schumann

Clarinet

PIANO CONCERTO IN A MINOR

1st Movement

E. Grieg

Allegro molto moderato. M. M. ♩ = 84.

Tutti Animato. M. M. ♩ = 108.

Tranquillo. ♩ = 80.

51

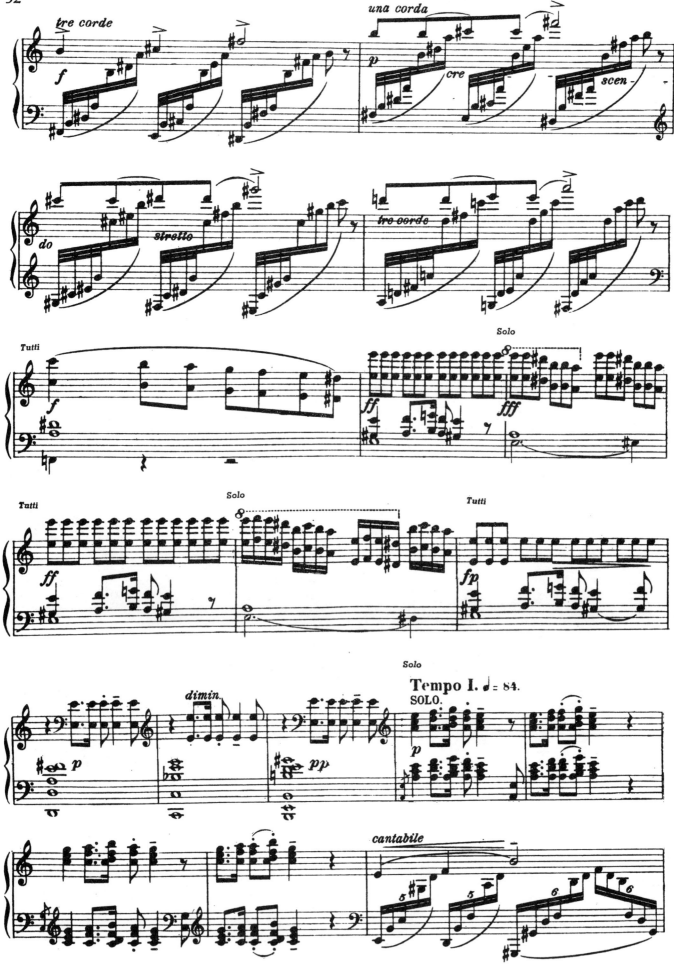

54

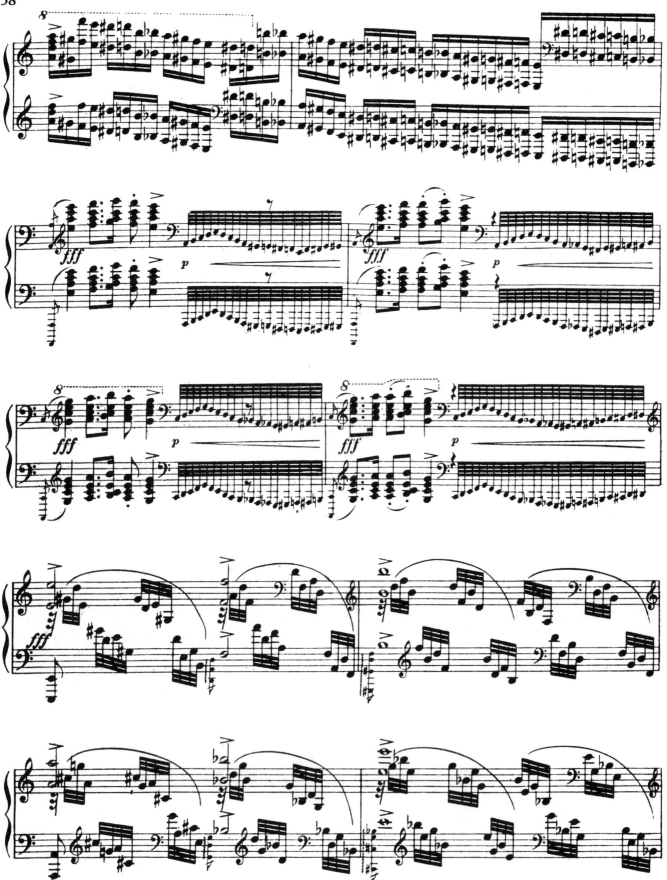

PIANO CONCERTO No. 1

In Bb Minor—1st Movement

(Condensed)

P. I. Tchaikovsky, Op. 23

Andante non troppo e molto maestoso.

64

68

PIANO CONCERTO No. 2

3rd Movement
(Condensed)

S. Rachmaninoff, Op. 18

74